# Were the Saints Astronauts? – A Transcendent View on the Exploration of the Universe

Rogerio Cietto

Published by Rogerio Cietto, 2024.

Were the saints astronauts? – A transcendent view on the exploration of the Universe

Published by Rogerio Paiva Cietto on Draft2Digital

*Raise your eyes and look at the heights.*
*Who created all this?*
*The one who sets in motion*
*every star of his heavenly host,*
*and calls everyone by name.*
*So great is your power*
*and his strength is so immense,*
*that none of them fail to attend!*
*Isaiah 40, 26*

# INDEX

# 1. INTRODUCTION

Christian, what is your hope? Pray to win the lottery? Work hard to create and maintain your family? Waiting for public authorities to solve all your problems? Escape from big cities and live in the countryside? Build an underground shelter and await the destruction of humanity? If any of these is your hope, you can sit tight, because your hope is vain and meaningless.

I explain. Or rather, I will let the Word of God explain your lack of hope. "How happy is he whose help is the God of Jacob, whose hope is in the Lord, in his God," Psalm 145 (146), 5. You are placing your hope in the things of this world, such as money, your individual effort, the material, scientific and technological progress of humanity. They are gifts from God to us, but they perish as the moth consumes it and the thief steals it, and they do not bring true hope.

Learn from the saints of the Church, who have stored up treasures in heaven and are there in eternal happiness and union with God. They simply followed the Divine Model of Our Lord Jesus Christ, Eternal Truth, Way of Salvation and Full Life. Of course, each of the saints had a different way of life, they were married or celibate, lived in poverty or were kings of great nations; all they had to do was live the Gospel well, simply and faithfully, defying the persecution, temptations and lusts that we all have to face.

Since the beginning of human history we have been challenged, and since Adam and Eve we have discovered the price of leaving the path suggested by God. With our first parents everything was good, since they had been created by God as we see in Genesis. But with the redemption by Jesus Christ we find an even better place, where we can go if we have waited devotedly and acted accordingly.

It turns out that scientific and technological progress, which we have experienced from the end of the 20th century to the present day, has made the vast majority of humanity believe that it is possible to achieve everything good in this world with sufficient knowledge and resources to spend in this regard.

In fact, we have made unimaginable progress in technique and science in the last fifty years. People believed that in our time we would have cures for all types of diseases, teleportation, (good) printed food and complete dominion over nature. Anyone who was a fan of Star Trek must remember the famous phrase:

*"Space, the final frontier. These are the voyages of the Starship Enterprise, on its mission to explore new worlds, seek out new lives and civilizations, going where no man has gone before."*

In practical terms, the proposal is: let's get together a group of people with a high degree of curiosity, willing to leave their families behind (or take them to space), risk their lives and spend their entire existence wandering around, searching for knowledge. This was their hope, to seek knowledge.

Now compare this motivation with that described by Pero Vaz de Caminha on Portugal's first arrival in Brazil, in the squadron led by Pedro Álvares Cabral:

*"However, the best result that can be taken from it seems to me to be saving these people. And this must be the main seed that Your Highness must sow in it. And if there was nothing more than having Your Highness here, this inn for this navigation of Calicut was enough. How much more, willingness to comply with it and do what Your Highness so desires, namely, adding to our faith!"*

(<http://www.dominiopublico.gov.br/download/texto/ua000283.pdf>)

The Great Navigations, in fact, yielded a lot of fruit, and I'm not talking about gold, brazilwood or spices. The Catholic faith reached all of America thanks to these brave pioneers, who faced the unknown, diseases, cannibalistic indigenous people and wild animals. They lost their lives, but they were seeking eternal life. Good deal.

We know the tree by its fruits (Luke 6, 44), and if today we have Saint Joseph of Anchieta, Saint Antonio de Sant'Anna Galvão, Saint Dulce of the Poors, Blessed Nhá Chica, Blessed Albertina Berkenbrock, Father Cícero, Father Leo and many pious souls who achieved the grace of eternal union with God were through this great undertaking in the New World.

Was it worth it?

*"Everything is worth it*
*If the soul is not small.*
*Who wants to go beyond Bojador*
*Has to go beyond the pain.*
*God gave the sea danger and the abyss,*
*But in it He mirrored the sky (heavens)*."*

Fernando Pessoa

*in Portuguese the word "*céu*" is used to refer to the sky (material) or to heavens (spiritual).

The person has to wonder: what fruits will our space exploration bring to humanity, without a supernatural purpose of saving souls? If we find intelligent life on other planets, what are we going to them for?

To gain knowledge? Wrong, if one day there is interstellar travel we will already be at such a level of knowledge that there would be no need to learn much from other civilizations.

To teach our knowledge? Also wrong, there is no point in risking our lives to propagate something that could be sent through a computer with a large screen, a powerful speaker and an automatic trigger sensor.

Explore new worlds as space tourism? Maybe, but who is going to risk their life on a journey lasting at least four and a half years, a very optimistic timeframe considering that one day we would be able to travel at the speed of light? Even if it is with current technology, and the trip is restricted to our solar system, would it be worth spending six months of your life just to get to the nearest planet?

None of these options seem very attractive to me, because it is not something that enhances the soul. This was the reason for the navigations, and if it is not with a supernatural intention of saving souls... unfortunately all this effort to reach space has no value in spiritual terms.

Of course you will say: the navigators didn't know what they would find! That's true. But in any case, the intention was to save their own souls, fulfilling the order that Our Lord made very clear before his ascension: "Go into the world and proclaim the Gospel to every creature" Mark 16, 15.

The Portuguese explorers did not even want to obtain knowledge, nor did they have the arrogance to think that they were going to teach things to other less evolved people. The intention was to ANNOUNCE ETERNAL TRUTHS, not scientific and technological development.

Now, does this mean that you defend that there are lives on other planets, and that we go there to evangelize them? Pay attention: I have no idea whether there is life on other planets or not, nor whether this life is intelligent enough to receive the good news from the Word of God, that is, possessing an immortal soul. However, I need to approach this matter as hypotheses, and nothing more than that.

In this humble work we will have many biblical and scientific quotes, so if you prefer to delve deeper into theological and technological issues, feel free to pause reading, confirm (or possibly refute) the information I am sharing, and return to your reading.

But let's be clear: the Catholic view of matters such as space travel and life on other planets must be in accordance with Catholic doctrine, the Church's magisterium and, without a doubt, the Word of God. In the words of Saint John Paul II:

"*Faith and reason (fides et ratio) constitute, as it were, the two wings by which the human spirit rises to the contemplation of truth*" (Encyclical *Fides et Ratio*).

Faith without reason is blind credulity, typical of pagans. Reason without faith is immanent skepticism, typical of atheists. My commitment, far from these two errors, is with the truth, at least with what God has allowed to be revealed to human beings up to now.

I just ask that you read until the end with an open heart and mind, even if you may not agree with everything that is written. In the end, you will certainly understand the reasoning and be able to better draw your conclusions.

# 2. THE ASCENSION OF JESUS AND THE ASSUMPTION OF MARY

*"After his suffering, Jesus presented himself to them and gave them* ***many indisputable evidence that he was alive.*** *He appeared to them for a period of forty days speaking to them about the Kingdom of God. On one occasion, while he was eating with them, he gave them this command: "Do not leave Jerusalem, but wait for the promise of my Father, which I spoke to you about. For John baptized with water, but within a few days you will be baptized with the Holy Spirit." Then those who were gathered together asked him, "Lord, are you going to restore the kingdom to Israel at this time?" He answered them, "It is not for you to know the times or dates that the Father has set by his own authority. But you will receive power when the Holy Spirit comes upon you, and you will be my witnesses in Jerusalem, in all Judea and Samaria, and to the ends of the earth." Having said this, he was lifted up on high as they looked, and a cloud hid him from their sight. And* ***they stared at the sky as he ascended.*** *Suddenly there appeared before them* ***two men dressed in white,*** *who said to them: "Galileans, why are you looking up to heaven? This same Jesus, who was taken up from you into heaven, will return in the same way as you saw him go up."* Acts of the Apostles 1, 3-11.

Every Christian, regardless of denomination, knows this passage well: after the Passion and Resurrection, Our Lord appears to the disciples with the final instructions: I am going, but I will send the Holy Spirit to guide each one in his apostolate, testifying with his life and with words everything that Jesus taught us.

From then on, it can be perceived that all human progress in the sciences (small letter) was the work of the Holy Spirit and the Gift of Knowledge (capital letter), which instigated the minds and hearts of many scientists and scholars about our existence, from the model from the atom to the movement of black holes.

There is no scientific knowledge without divine inspiration, and the closer we are to living eternal truths, in imitation of our Lord and Savior, the more we know the truths of this world.

I want to draw attention to two specific excerpts from this passage. In verses 9 to 11 (in bold) it is clear that Jesus ascended to heaven in body and spirit, and remains there to this day, according to the two angels (men dressed in white is a euphemism to facilitate understanding).

Take into account the depth of this text: the body of Jesus is in the eternal home with the Father, intact and very much alive. If this were not the case, there would be no point in raising Our Lord's holy body into space, only for it to turn into cosmic dust.

Jesus' own words confirm this reality "*In my Father's house are many mansions; if it weren't so, I would have told you. I will prepare a place for you.*" John 14, 2. In other words, there is a place up there, waiting for us, being built according to our faith (verse 1) and our works (verse 12).

We contemplate this eternal truth in the Creed ("*he ascended into heaven and is seated at the right hand of the Father*") and in the second glorious mystery of the Holy Rosary (The Ascension of Jesus Christ). For more than two thousand years, atheists and Pharisees everywhere have been looking for the body of Jesus Christ to try to prove that the Christian faith is a sham, that Christ is not God.

If this is your case, you can stop reading this book and go look for it. Everyone who really tried came back with even stronger faith. Furthermore, the remission of our sins occurred with the sacrifice of the Paschal Lamb, and the resurrection was just proof that everything was being fulfilled in accordance with the Holy Scriptures, through the prophets Isaiah and Jeremiah, for example. More than 300 prophecies fulfilled through the same person, a probability of 1 in $10^{170}$ (10 followed by 170 zeros).

Likewise, Our Lady's immaculate body is also occupying a special place in the eternal abode. She who was born without sin, lived without sin and died without sin, would have no compatible place in this corrupt world. We contemplate this eternal truth in the fourth glorious mystery of the Holy Rosary, as it is a dogma of the Church and of which there is no further discussion.

Saint Thomas, the same one who doubted the Resurrection of Christ until he stuck his finger in His Wounds, was also the only apostle who did not see and did not believe in the Assumption of Our Lady into heaven, but who later opened Our Lady's tomb and found only lilies and roses, and Our Holy Mother appeared to Thomas from heaven and presented him with her maternal belt. (https://padrepauloricardo.org/blog/a-reliquia-do-cinto-de-nossa-senhora).

Relics can be found that prove the existence of these miracles, but for those who don't want to believe, not all the proof in the world is enough.

However, for those who want to believe, but are not fooled by any wind of false doctrine, it can be concluded that Our Lord and Our Lady are in one place, waiting for us. Our Lady even comes to call us to this great festival of eternal happiness with God, like in La Salette, Lourdes, Fátima, Akita, Quibeho... (you can be sure that she didn't come here to do tourism). Now let's look at some who definitely made it there.

# 3. MILACLES OF INCORRUPT BODIES

The reality of the incorrupt bodies of Our Lord Jesus Christ and Our Blessed Mother is, on the one hand, a dogma of the Catholic Church and a topic that has no place for discussion or contrary opinion. Whoever had no sin, since he was born without the stain of original sin, would not suffer from the corruption of the flesh, which affected the entire human body due to the spiritual inheritance received from Adam and Eve.

Thus, in addition to Our Lord and Our Lady having ascended to heaven, as explained in the previous chapter, they are still there, in one piece, because they cannot have suffered any influence from the sin of our first parents. Otherwise, it wouldn't make any sense to send a holy body to the highest heavens, if upon reaching its destination it started to rot.

However, how can we prove to the most skeptical that the bodies of Jesus and Mary did not suffer decomposition or deterioration due to chemical and biological agents? In this case, we can provide indirect proof, from people who lived in this world with such an odor of holiness, that their bodies (or a specific part of them) remain intact even after many years of death, and even after being exposed to various hazardous conditions.

Some important details about holiness: first, many people died in the odor of holiness, because they had lived some virtue in a heroic way, but they did not necessarily have a reputation for holiness during their lives or immediately after death. True spiritual progress is internal, and the external is a consequence, according to Saint Maximilian Maria Kolbe, a modern martyr.

Second, when the Catholic Church recognizes that a person is a saint, it is because the life and miracles performed through them have been duly verified, studied by scientists, the process of beatification and subsequent canonization goes through the Congregation for the Causes of Saints, to authenticate the holiness of that individual.

Therefore, there may indeed be many saints in heaven that the Church does not officially recognize, because those who lived holiness well spent their lives loving God above all things, without needing to post their charity or any good deed on social media. He lived exactly what Jesus asked: do good works in secret, and the Father in Heaven will give you the due reward. May your right hand not know what my left hand is doing (Matthew 6:3).

However, those who passed through the sieve and were recognized to be elevated to the glory of the altars are in fact saints, in the strict sense of the term. You can trust, because the authority of the Church in making such a declaration is based on the Holy Spirit of God himself, who will never abandon Peter and his successors (Matthew 16, 18).

Without a doubt, we have many types of saints throughout the history of humanity. Even though they suffered from original sin and concupiscence, they knew how to make themselves perfectly suited to God's will, loving God above all things and loving others as Christ loved us.

It turns out that some saints received an extraordinary gift from God, which reflects precisely what we are talking about, about making it difficult for nature to act on that pile of cells from falling apart and the body from becoming a pile of dust. Escaping (even if in part) the Universe's entire tendency towards entropy (disaggregation of matter), it is the miracle of incorruptible bodies.

There are many false ideas about this type of miracle, so it is worth making an important statement right away: to configure the miracle of the incorrupt body, it is not necessary for the corpse to be completely preserved, but for it to show signs of conservation that are very unusual, even after having the saint's tomb had been opened, and had not undergone any artificial preservation process, such as embalming.

Thus, a body kept in a vacuum for hundreds of years would naturally be preserved, but at the time of its opening and exposure it would quickly decompose. It's not a miracle, since there's nothing supernatural about it. Very dry and cold environments are also conducive to the natural preservation of bodies.

Some examples of saints whose bodies were considered incorrupt:

- Bernardette Soubirous, the French clairvoyant of the famous apparition of Our Lady of the Immaculate Conception, in Lourdes;

- Catarina Labouré, another French clairvoyant, from the famous apparition of Our Lady of Graces of the Miraculous Medal, on Rue do Bac, Paris;

- Padre Pio of Pietrelcina, the Capuchin friar with countless prodigies such as bilocation, dialogue with guardian angels, xenolalia (he spoke a dialect from Italy and people understood English, French, etc.), received the stigmata of Christ and performed inexplicable cures for medicine to this day;

- Saint Zita of Lucca, patroness saint of domestic workers, whose body was found intact three hundred years after her death, and who, even after being exposed, still has her internal organs, including her lungs, seriously affected by the soot from her workplace;

- Saint John Maria Vianney, the Curé of Ars, hero of the confessionals, who acquired his fame for spending up to 18 hours attending to penitents;

- Saint Charbel Makhlouf, a monk from Lebanon who continued to shed blood from his body even fifty years after his death.

There is also the hypothesis of the incorrupt bodies of Saint Joseph, the nurturing father of Jesus, and Saint John the Baptist, purified in the womb of Saint Elizabeth during the visit of Our Lady shortly after the annunciation of the angel Gabriel. However, there are no official documents regarding these cases.

One can only suppose that, if it is possible to find the remains of almost all the apostles (who died at the same time as these two saints), it would also be possible to find the remains of John the Baptist and Joseph, if they had become corrupt. But let's be clear that this is just a hypothesis!

Other saints had only part of their bodies considered incorrupt, such as:

- the heart of Saint Vincent de Paul, the man who lived charity and love for the poor in a heroic way (it is also there on Rue du Bac);

- the left hand of Saint Tereza de Ávila, doctor of the Church, who wrote, among others, The Book of Life and Interior Castle;

- the language of Saint Anthony of Padua, whose preaching made even the fish and birds stop to pay attention to the proclamation of the Gospel.

If these saints had their bodies kept intact, it is a sign that they lived a holy life, and at the time of the resurrection from the dead (at the second coming of Jesus), they will already be in the process of inhabiting their bodies again. Note well: IT IS NOT REINCARNATION, when a body was assigned to a soul it only inhabits it.

If even with the corruption of original sin these bodies (or part of them) managed to remain well preserved, imagine the glorious bodies of Jesus Christ, the Word of God made Flesh and of Immaculate Mary, whose graces are greater than that of all angels and saints. Together.

Is it enough for you to believe in the resurrection of the dead? We will return to this topic in a moment.

# 4. PRODIGY OF THE EXALTATION OF THE SPIRIT

What is gravity? So well known in our daily lives that we don't even remember it, the force of gravity consists of a force of attraction on bodies, forming a gravitational field.

Gravity is one of the four fundamental forces existing in nature. The others are the electromagnetic interaction force, the weak nuclear force and the strong nuclear force. This force is responsible for defining the weight of a body, a vertical and downward vector that prevents people and things from flying off the planet due to the Earth's rotation.

We can check and compare gravity only between planets and celestial bodies, such as the Moon, the Sun, planets, their satellites and stars, since even the most obese person on the planet will not be able to attract even an insect into their personal orbit. Gravity is for the big ones only.

The Earth has a mass of just $5{,}9 \times 10^{24}$ kg, which is more than enough to make your feet stick to the floor. The Sun, for example, weighs approximately $1{,}98 \times 10^{33}$ kg (thirty-three zeros), and is not even the largest in our known universe, but it manages to keep several small planets around it.

It turns out that gravity is the only force that science and technology still do not have the slightest grasp of, it only knows how to observe and calculate, based on the mass and distance between bodies. Compare: magnetism and its implications (electromagnetism) are used freely in every lamp and household appliance; the strong nuclear force is manipulated by atomic fission and fusion, with medical and military applications, and many others; the weak nuclear force is more peaceful and easier to use, as with the decay of particles we use radiation for various purposes.

Of course you might think: balloons, space rockets and artificial satellites dominate gravity. Negative! None of these can generate an anti-gravity force, only a contrary kinetic force that nullifies the effects of gravity. Geostationary satellites, for example, are always moving in parallel to the Earth's globe, to generate a centrifugal (kinetic) force away from the Earth, in a way that counteracts gravity, which insists on continuing to work.

All this scientific explanation was necessary to understand the miracle known as EXALTATION OF THE SPIRIT. In this extraordinary event, the saint's connection with God is so intense that they hover in the air, as if they were a balloon or a helicopter, but without any scientific explanation for the phenomenon.

Note well: the saint who experiences this miracle does not become lighter than air, like a helium balloon. It does not even suffer the effects of aerodynamic force, which causes objects heavier than air to fly through the pressure difference in their wings or propellers. There is no driving force behind a massive release of gases, as in a firecracker or rocket, that propels the saint in a certain direction. It can fill a human being's entire stomach with methane gas (eating enough sweet potatoes, cabbage, beans, etc.) that he will not be able to rise into the air, and even the combustion of these gases would not make the person rise a millimeter off the ground.

It is known that a large number of saints levitated, including Saint Teresa of Ávila, Padre Pio, Saint Martin de Porres, Saint Francis of Assisi, Saint Anthony of Padua, Saint Philip Neri, Saint Alphonsus of Ligório and the most famous in this regard, Saint Joseph of Cupertino, patron saint of aviators and astronauts. The latter had such an exaltation of spirit that his companions had to tie a rope around his waist during processions with the Blessed Sacrament, to prevent him from being lost in the air.

G. K. Chesterton said that "angels can fly because they don't take themselves too seriously (literally, they take life lightly)". The same can be said of Saint Joseph of Cupertino. He didn't take himself too seriously; he was humble, that's why he didn't weigh so much; it defied gravity because it was light; he levitated thanks to his lightness of spirit.

Of course, this phenomenon is not isolated: all these saints had an extraordinary spiritual and ascetic life, mystical experiences, divine revelations, but the most important thing was a deep intimacy with God and a complete, unrestricted and irrevocable detachment from the things of this world.

Without a doubt, modern man prefers to trust in a drone capable of supporting his weight and transporting him anywhere he wants much more than this type of miracle. This person unfortunately does not believe in any miracles, and if you fit this profile, you are not interested in reading this book. I hope you have a personal encounter with God one day, and that this encounter occurs under favorable circumstances (which is not always the case).

Miracles exist, we don't need faith for them to occur, but to see them and understand that God's hand is clearly acting at that moment (He is always acting in our lives, but most of the time Our Lord is discreet and does the miracle without us noticing).

In the same way that some saints experienced this preternatural phenomenon, people possessed by evil spirits also suffer various inexplicable events, such as climbing walls, strength beyond what humans are capable of, and even speaking foreign languages without ever having studied. The spiritual world is all around you, you just need to tune in to your soul and spirit.

Many people have difficulty believing in these types of phenomena described in the lives of some saints, but they see no obstacle in believing that advanced civilizations are able to abduct people into spaceships, talk to them and even give them some tips on health, well-being and even financial investments. They are those who call themselves "spiritual but not religious".

For these I have very simple evangelical advice: "You will know the truth, and the truth will set you free" (John 8:32). Only eternal truth frees us from false doctrines and pseudo-religions. Modern man wants to change the world so he doesn't have to change himself. The saint, on the contrary, doesn't care much about the world, what he wants is to accumulate the treasures of heaven (Matthew 6:19), that is, spiritual goods that far exceed mere scientific knowledge or material progress.

Because that must have been what these saints did: they imitated Christ in such a way, with such perfection and humility, with such joy and lightness of spirit even in the most unfavorable circumstances, that they entered into tune with Him and detached themselves from this world, in such a way point that they gave their souls to the Eternal and allowed themselves to be attracted by Him.

This force, which attracts us to God, is so far the only one that has managed to nullify the force of gravity, a fact that no device or technique has been capable of to date, and probably never will be. This is the strength that takes us to heaven, to the eternal home that Jesus Christ has for us.

This is the path, the way to get to heaven. So, do you want to go there or not?

# 5. IS HEAVEN A PLACE OR A CONDITION OF THE SOUL?

This theme requires a deep and fundamental analysis to grow in faith, followed in Catholic theology, addressing not only the nature of heaven as the final destination of the faithful, but also the spiritual experience and transformation of the soul. This chapter explores Catholic perspectives on this issue, drawing on Church doctrine, Scripture, and tradition.

For the Catholic Church, heaven is described as the definitive state of perfect happiness, full communion with God and complete fulfillment of the human being. It is a state of eternal existence where the righteous enjoy the presence of God in its fullness. This concept transcends the mere idea of a physical place and enters the scope of a spiritual and transcendent reality.

The traditional Catholic view does not simply consider heaven as a physical location in space, but emphasizes its spiritual and supernatural nature. According to the Catechism of the Catholic Church (number 1024), "heaven is the blessed communion of life and love with the Holy Trinity, with the Virgin Mary, the angels and all the blessed". This suggests that heaven is more than a simple geographic space, but a spiritual reality where God's presence is fully manifested and experienced.

The basis of the Catholic understanding of heaven is found in Holy Scripture, especially in the teachings of Jesus Christ. In John 14, 2 to 3, Jesus promises his disciples that he will prepare places for them in the Father's house, indicating the idea of a place prepared for those who faithfully follow Him. Furthermore, passages such as Revelation 21 vividly describe a heavenly new Jerusalem, adorned like a bride prepared for her husband, who symbolizes the perfect union between God and his people.

Although heaven is conceived as a state of communion with God, Catholic tradition also emphasizes that this communion implies a profound transformation of the soul. It is not just about being in one place, but about a fullness of life in God that completely transcends earthly limitations. This transformation involves the purification of the soul in purgatory, for those who need it, and entry into the divine presence in a complete and immortal way.

Therefore, for the Catholic faith, heaven is not just a physical place, but a state of full communion with God, experienced by the souls of the righteous after death. It is a spiritual reality where eternal happiness and divine presence are experienced in a complete and transformative way. This understanding not only consoles the faithful in the face of mortality, but also inspires a life of faith, hope and charity, in the search for holiness that culminates in the fullness of eternal life in heaven.

From what has already been explained in the previous chapters, it is clear that the place called Heaven, Eternal House, Celestial Glory, Eternal Life, is a place, which occupies a specific region in existence. It is also a state of communion with God, but beyond that it is a physical space, which many people reach, the saints of God.

First of all, we need to remember that heaven has to do with bodies, which are undeniably material. Now, being materials has to do with space. Therefore, it is not possible to completely dismiss the statement that heaven is not a place. Man is a creature of God, made up of body and soul. Thus, since heaven is God's communion with man, it is not possible to exclude his body.

Communion between God and man exists from now on, in the person of Jesus Christ, whose body was resurrected and transformed, as seen in the Gospel of Saint Luke:

"*While they were still talking about these things, Jesus stood among them and said to them: Peace be with you! Disturbed and amazed, they thought they were seeing a spirit. But He said to them: Why are you troubled, and why do you have these doubts in your hearts? See my hands and my feet, it is I myself; feel and see: a spirit does not have flesh and bones, as you see I have. And when he had said this, he showed them his hands and his feet. But while they were still hesitating and were filled with joy, he asked: Do you have anything to eat here? Then they offered him a piece of roasted fish. He took and ate in their sight.*" (Luke 24:36-43)

In heaven, in addition to the body of Our Lord Jesus Christ, there is also the body of his Holy Mother. Yes, she was elevated to heavenly glory body and soul, as seen in the Apostolic Constitution of Pope Pius XII, *Munificentissimus Deus*, which precisely defined the dogma of the assumption of body and soul into heaven, which says:

*"44. "Therefore, after having made repeated supplications to God, and having invoked the peace of the Spirit of truth, to the glory of the omnipotent God who granted his special benevolence to the virgin Mary, in honor of his Son, the immortal King of ages and triumphant of sin and death, to increase the glory of his august mother, and for the joy and joy of the whole Church, with the authority of our Lord Jesus Christ, of the blessed apostles Saint Peter and Saint Paul and with Ours, we pronounce, declare and define to be a divinely revealed dogma that: the Immaculate Mother of God, the ever-virgin Mary, having completed the course of her earthly life, was assumed body and soul into heavenly glory."*

At the end of time, all creation - transformed - will be united with God. This is stated in the Catechism of the Catholic Church, in number 1060:

*"At the end of time, the Kingdom of God will reach its fullness. Then, the righteous will reign with Christ forever, glorifying in body and soul and the material universe itself will be transformed. Then God will be 'all in all', in Eternal Life."*

The Catechism also presents, from numbers 1042 to 1050, the concept of **palingenesis**, that is, the new generation of the universe, which Saint Peter describes as "*the new heavens and the new earth*" (2 Pet 3, 13). There is a relationship between man's eternal happiness and the universe. God created man from clay, breathed his Spirit upon him, commanded him to multiply and dominate the earth:

"*Then God said, 'Let us make man in our image and likeness. May he reign over the fish of the sea, over the birds of the sky, over the livestock, over all the earth, and over every creeping thing that creeps on the earth." God created man in his own image; he created him in the In the image of God, he created man and woman. God blessed them: "Be fruitful, he said, and multiply, fill the earth and subdue it. Rule over the fish of the sea, over the birds of the sky, and over every living creature that moves on the earth." God said, "Behold, I give you every herb that yields seed on the earth, and every fruit tree that They contain their seed within themselves, so that they may be food for you.*" (Genesis 1:26-29)

Thus, the world belongs to man, who must dominate it, according to the will of God. This does not mean, at all, that man can destroy nature, because God is the Creator of everything and, out of respect for Him, it is not possible to tarnish what He has made. However, the relationship between God and man was disturbed by sin. The same sacred book metaphorically explains the rupture that occurred:

"*And he said to the man, "Because you listened to your wife's voice and ate fruit from the tree that I prohibited you from eating, cursed be the ground because of you. You will take your sustenance from her with painful labor all the days of your life. It will produce thorns and thistles for you, and you will eat the grass of the land. You shall eat your bread by the sweat of your face until you return to the land from which you were taken; for you are dust, and to dust you will return.*" (Genesis 3:17-19)

The harmony between humans and the cosmos was disturbed by sin. Now, Jesus is the Redeemer and came to redeem this stumble. Therefore, Saint Paul says to the Romans:

"*I consider that the sufferings of this present life bear no proportion to the future glory that must be manifested to us. Therefore, the creation eagerly awaits the manifestation of the children of God. For the creation was subjected to vanity (not voluntarily, but by the will of him who subjected her), yet with the hope of being freed from the captivity of corruption, to participate in the glorious freedom of the children of God, for we know that the whole creation groans and suffers as in labor pains until this day. Not only it, but also we, who have the firstfruits of the Spirit, groan within ourselves, awaiting the adoption, the redemption of our body."* (Romans 8, 18-23)

There will, therefore, be '*new heavens and a new earth*' (cf. 2 Pet 3:13) and, thus, it cannot be said that heaven - full and perfect communion with God - will be something completely outside the notions of space and place. However, because it is a regeneration, a transfiguration of the universe, it means that the concept of place and space, although it has to do with this new world, does not fully express what it will be. It is a mystery.

After the resurrection, Jesus entered and left places, passed through doors, ate and drank, as we read in the aforementioned account from the Gospel of Luke, therefore, he was a presence, a transformed body, different from human reality. Cardinal Ratzinger, in his Manual of Eschatology – Death and Eternal Life, says: "*Heaven cannot be given a topographical definition nor can it be placed inside or outside our structure of space. However, it cannot even be separated trying to make it simply a state, a situation, cannot be totally separated from the whole of the cosmos. In reality, we are talking here about a universal power that belongs to the new 'space of the body of Christ', the space of the communion of saints.*"

There will be a new space, a new concept of place, of which there is no experience, therefore, simply saying that there is no such place is inaccurate, in the same way that saying that there is a place that has already been experienced is also inaccurate. In the face of mystery, theological reflection can help, however, to really understand what heaven is, it is necessary to resort to communion with God, with the Body of Christ. How this will happen is not possible to specify, but it can already be mysteriously experienced here on Earth through the sacrament of the Eucharist.

Eucharistic communion allows an experience of a new concept of space, because in each host Christ is present as a whole, in each fragment He is totally present, because it is not a spatial presence, but a substantial presence. And so, it touches each person spiritually, but also physically.

In the Eucharist begins the experience of the new place that is heaven and the new earth, a new space, a new cosmos. In the Eucharistic Bread and Wine the cosmos has been transformed where Christ is now the all in all.

# 6. WHAT CAN WE AFFIRM ABOUT THE RESURRECTION OF THE DEAD?

The resurrection of the dead is one of the central pillars of the Catholic faith, reflecting a deep hope in life after death and God's promise to restore and renew all things at the end of time. In this chapter we will explore the meaning, biblical basis and the Catholic Church's belief in the resurrection of the dead.

For Catholics, the resurrection of the dead is not just an abstract theological concept, but a fundamental reality that sustains their hope and faith. It refers to the belief that at the end of time, all who have died will be resurrected with transformed and glorified bodies. This means that it is not simply about returning to earthly life as it was before death, but about being renewed in a glorious and eternal form, as described in 1st Corinthians 15, 42-44.

The basis of Catholic belief in the resurrection of the dead is firmly rooted in Holy Scripture. Jesus Christ, the Son of God, rose from the dead as the first of the resurrected, thus inaugurating new life for all those who believe in Him. His own resurrection is witnessed in the gospels and is the cornerstone of the Christian faith. Saint Paul, in his letters, also explains in detail the nature of the resurrection and its meaning for the faithful.

Furthermore, several passages in the Old Testament also prefigure the resurrection of the dead, such as the visions of the prophets Ezekiel (Ez 37) and Daniel (Dn 12), which speak of the restoration of Israel and eternal life.

The Catholic Church teaches that all human beings will be resurrected on the last day, when Christ returns in glory. This doctrine is included in the Nicenoconstantinopolitan Creed, which many Catholics profess regularly during the liturgy. The Catechism of the Catholic

Church also teaches that the resurrection of the dead is a real event and is closely linked to divine justice and the fullness of the Kingdom of God.

Believing in the resurrection of the dead has significant implications for the lives of Catholics here and now. Firstly, it offers comfort and hope in the face of death, as eternal life with God is promised to those who live in communion with Him. Furthermore, it guides Christian ethics and morality, encouraging the faithful to live righteously and godly lives, knowing that your actions will have eternal consequences.

In short, the resurrection of the dead is a central dogma of the Catholic faith, based on the promise of God revealed in Scripture and taught by the Church over the centuries. It offers hope, comfort and a deep sense of meaning to the lives of Christians, reminding them that death is not the end, but rather the beginning of a full and eternal life with God.

The Catholic Church has dogmatic formulas containing the main elements of its faith and are used in both the Liturgy and Catechesis, the so-called "symbols". Therefore, the following expression is found in the Apostolic Symbol: "I believe [...] in the resurrection of the flesh..." and in the Nicene-Constantinopolitan Symbol: "[...] And I hope for the resurrection of the dead... ", therefore, both expressions are appropriate.

The Congregation for the Doctrine of the Faith noted that in some missals in different parts of the world the word "flesh" was replaced by "body". To remedy this, in December 1983, under the presidency of the then Cardinal Ratzinger, he published the document "Decisions on the translation of the article 'Carnis Resurrectionem' of the Apostolic Symbol", in which he requested that all Episcopal Conferences adopt the literal translation of what it is "resurrection of the flesh" and not others, even if similar.

The subject is quite complex, as there is a theological current that insists on the error of maintaining that there is a resurrection immediately after death. Who has never, during a wake or in homilies, heard that the person being veiled has already been resurrected. It is commonplace, but inadequate, as the Church teaches that the resurrection will only occur at the end of time.

The Church, when affirming the resurrection of the flesh, is being clearer and more precise in the fact that the flesh inside the coffin will be resurrected on the last day. On March 17, 1979, the Congregation for the Doctrine of the Faith published a letter dealing with "issues relating to eschatology", cited below:

*"This Sacred Congregation, responsible for promoting and protecting the doctrine of faith, wants here to remember what the Church in the name of Christ teaches, especially regarding what happens between the Christian's death and the universal resurrection.*

*1. The Church believes in the resurrection of the dead.*

*2. The Church understands that the resurrection refers to the whole man; for the elect, it is nothing other than the extension of Christ's own resurrection to men.*

*3. The Church affirms the continuation and subsistence, after death, of a spiritual element endowed with consciousness and will, so that in the intervening time the 'human self' itself exists, but lacking the complement of the body. To designate this element, the Church uses the term 'soul', consecrated by the use of Sacred Scripture and Tradition. Although it is not unaware that this term has different meanings in the Bible, it believes, however, that no valid reason can be given to reject it and, at the same time, he believes that a term of language is absolutely necessary to support the faith of Christians.*

*4. The Church excludes any form of thought or expression that makes its way of praying, its funeral rites, its worship of the dead absurd or unintelligible - realities that, substantially, constitute theological places.*

*5. The Church, in accordance with the Holy Scriptures, awaits 'the glorious manifestation of our Lord Jesus Christ', which, moreover, she believes is distinct and ulterior in comparison with the condition of men immediately after death.*

*6. The Church, in its teaching on the condition of man after death, excludes, however, any explanation that empties the meaning of the Assumption of the Virgin Mary in its unique meaning; namely, in this sense, that the bodily glorification of the Virgin is the anticipation of the glorification reserved for all the elect.*

*7. The Church, in faithful adherence to the New Testament and Tradition, believes in the happiness of the righteous who will one day be in Christ. It believes in the eternal punishment that awaits the sinner, who will be deprived of the vision of God, and in the repercussion of this punishment on his entire being. Finally, it believes that for the elect there may be an eventual purification prior to the divine vision, totally different, however, from the punishment of the condemned. This is what the Church understands when it talks about hell and purgatory.*

*When it comes to the condition of man after death, it is necessary to be especially careful about the danger of arbitrary representations based solely on imagination, as their excesses form an important part of the difficulties that the Christian faith often encounters. The images used by Holy Scripture, however, deserve respect. It is necessary to understand their deep meaning, avoiding the danger of attenuating them too much, as this often means emptying the realities that these images represent of their content.*

*Neither Holy Scripture nor theologians provide sufficient light for an adequate description of life after death. Christian believers must firmly maintain these two essential points: on the one hand, believe in the fundamental continuity existing, by virtue of the Holy Spirit, between the present life in Christ and the future life (for charity is the law of the kingdom of God, and by our charity exercised on earth our participation in divine glory in heaven will be measured); but, on the other hand, the Christian must be aware of the radical rupture that exists between the present life and the future, since the economy of faith is replaced by the economy of full light, and we will be in Christ and 'see God'; and in these promises and mystery our hope essentially consists. If the imagination cannot reach there, the heart arrives instinctively and in depth."* (DH 4650-

4659) <https://padrepauloricardo.org/episodios/ressurreicao-dos-mortos-ou-ressurreicao-da-carne>.

It can be seen that the document above is clear about the Catholic belief that there will only be a resurrection at the end of time, that it will not be a metaphor, but will include the body and soul of the individual. How this will happen is something the human mind cannot even imagine.

In 1990, the International Theological Commission, one of the branches of the Congregation for the Doctrine of the Faith, published an opinion called "Some current questions of eschatology", which states that the resurrection will only take place in the so-called **Parousia**, that is, at the second coming of Jesus Christ, in a historical and future event, taking down the teachings of modernist theologians.

Finally, the Church makes it clear that, of all creatures, only the Holy Mary was resurrected, in the so-called "Assumption". All other human beings are waiting for the return of Jesus Christ, although we know that the resurrection of us all, in the end, is achieved by the resurrection of Christ himself, the source of the resurrection of all the dead and living. Everyone will be body and soul in the glory of God, which is why we believe in the resurrection of the dead or resurrection of the flesh.

# 7. THEORY OF INTELLIGENT DESIGN

The origin of life on Earth is one of the greatest and most intriguing scientific mysteries. The quest to understand how life emerged on our planet involves several areas of knowledge, including biology, chemistry, physics and even philosophy. From scientific theories to philosophical and theological approaches, there are several proposed explanations for the complex phenomenon of the origin of life. In this chapter, we will explore the main theories that try to explain how life emerged on Earth.

The theory of **abiogenesis**, also known as the "spontaneous origin of life", suggests that life arose from non-living matter by natural processes. This theory is based on the idea that complex organic molecules can form from simpler chemical compounds, eventually leading to the development of living organisms.

In 1953, Stanley Miller and Harold Urey performed a famous experiment that simulated conditions on early Earth. They were able to synthesize amino acids, the building blocks of proteins, by passing electrical discharges through a mixture of gases believed to be present in the early atmosphere. This experiment provided evidence that organic compounds essential for life could form abiogenically. <https://www.ufrgs.br/astronomia/wp-content/uploads/2018/04/Explorando_S5_J_Eduardo_Exobiologia.pdf>.

The RNA world model proposes that early life used RNA as genetic material, before DNA and proteins evolved. RNA is capable of storing genetic information and also acting as a catalyst, making it a good candidate for the first living systems.

The theory of **panspermia** suggests that life on Earth may have originated from biological material (such as spores or microorganisms) that came from outside the planet, brought by meteorites, comets or space dust. This theory does not address how life arose, but rather how it may have been transported to Earth (DAVIES, Paul. The Fifth Miracle, pg. 94).

The **Lithographic Panspermia**, a variant of panspermia, proposes that space rocks, such as meteorites, could have transported microorganisms or precursors of life to Earth.

On the other hand, the **Cosmic Panspermia** suggests that the seeds of life could have come from a more distant source, such as another star or galaxy, instead of just the Solar System.

The **Creation theory**, although not scientific, is an important perspective, especially in theological and religious contexts. It holds that life was created by a divine entity or supernatural force. Different religious traditions offer varying explanations about the origin of life. I clarify that the passage from Genesis 1 should not be read literally, but as symbolism characteristic of the historical moment in which the book was written (that is, without current scientific knowledge).

In Christianity, the origin of life is attributed to God, who created all things as described in the Book of Genesis. Life is seen as an act of direct divine creation. He is the Efficient Cause, which has no antecedent; only He could generate the Universe with love and keep it in balance.

Other religious traditions also have their own explanations about the creation of life, generally involving the action of gods or higher entities.

Another approach suggests that life could have originated in specific environments, such as underwater hot springs, where chemical conditions are favorable for the formation of complex organic molecules. Hydrothermal vents at the bottom of the oceans provide an environment rich in minerals and energy, which could have facilitated the synthesis of molecules essential for life.

The **hydrothermal springs** hypothesis proposes that life could have begun in underwater environments rich in chemical compounds and thermal energy. These places could have provided the necessary conditions for the formation and maintenance of the first life forms.

The **chlorophyllosome world** theory suggests that early life may have originated in formations of chlorophyllosomes, submicroscopic structures that may have facilitated the conversion of solar energy into chemical energy before the formation of complex cells.

The origin of life on Earth is a multifaceted topic that continues to generate intense research and debate. Theories range from the spontaneous formation of complex organic compounds, to the possibility of life coming from outside the planet, without ruling out that, in any case, life is the result of divine action. Each theory offers a unique perspective, and despite scientific advances, the mystery of the origin of life has not yet been completely solved. The integration of these ideas and continued scientific exploration promise to further illuminate this fascinating aspect of our existence.

The Theory of Intelligent Design (TDI) has sparked intense debates in recent decades, especially in the field of science and philosophy. Advocated by many as a valid approach to explaining the irreducible complexity and specified information found in nature, TDI finds particular resonance within the perspective of the Catholic faith.

The Catholic faith, grounded in divine revelation and reason, offers a rich context for understanding and supporting the central principles of TDI. The core of this Theory lies in the fact that certain aspects of the universe and living beings are best explained by an intelligent cause, in contrast to purely natural or random processes. This concept resonates with the Catholic belief in an intelligent Creator, who is both the source and sustainer of all creation.

Catholic doctrine emphasizes the harmony between faith and reason, highlighting that scientific knowledge and understanding of faith should not be seen as mutually exclusive, but rather as complementary. Saint John Paul II, in his encyclical *Fides et Ratio*, highlighted the importance of a reason open to transcendence, capable of investigating both natural causes and final causes and, thus, recognizing signs of intelligent design in creation.

TDI proposes that certain biological and physical phenomena are highly unlikely to have arisen through mere random processes and that they exhibit characteristics that point to intelligent intervention. For Catholic thought, this aligns with the idea that God, as the omnipotent and omniscient Creator, may have organized nature in ways that reflect his own wisdom and intelligence.

Several examples in nature have been cited as evidence of intelligent design, such as the complexity of cellular structures, the highly organized genetic code and biological systems that exhibit precise and interdependent adaptations. TDI suggests that these characteristics are best explained by a creative mind that planned and executed these complex systems.

A good observer is able to find the divine signature in fractals, for example. These seemingly random and non-linear geometric shapes are often found in nature, such as a snowflake. How is a crystal organized so that the fractions (fractals) repeat the traits and appearance of the complete whole?

The Fibonacci sequence is another example. Start with the first natural number (1) and continue adding the antecedent: (1), 1+1 (2), 2+1 (3), 3+2 (5), 5+3 (8), 8+5 ( 13), 13+8, (21), 21+13 (34), 34+21 (55), and so on. This apparently random sum is found, for example, in the shape of shells, in the leaves of trees, in the waves of the sea. How is it possible that all the shells in the oceans have the same proportion?

For me, God's signature is visible on the Periodic Table of Elements. God created the Universe so precisely that all its atomic bricks have their right place. You don't need to be an expert in chemistry to see that there is no empty place in the sequence of atomic numbers (number of protons in the nucleus). After Copper (29) comes Zinc (30). Before Sulfur (16) comes Phosphorus (15).

When chemist Dmitri Mendeleev began organizing the Periodic Table as we know it, in 1869, he noticed that certain atomic numbers were missing for some elements. However, instead of putting everything together and assuming that some atomic numbers had "jumped" in order (i.e., the corresponding elements, such as Aluminum (13) and Phosphorus (15) did not exist), this brilliant scientist believed that there were order in the created Universe and left the spaces vacant in the Table, stating that there were chemical elements that had not yet been discovered.

Mendeleev believed there was order in chaos, a profound act of faith in a Creator who would not make things messy. Even though Chemistry was the terror of my high school years, I actually started to like the subject after learning about it.

From a Catholic perspective, the TDI approach is not only consistent with the vision of a God who acts through creation, but also respects the freedom of scientific inquiry. The Catholic Church encourages the diligent study of nature as a means of better understanding the divine wisdom manifested in the created world.

In addition to its scientific implications, TDI raises profound philosophical and theological issues. It questions the adequacy of purely materialist explanations for the origin and development of life and the universe, promoting reflection on the purpose and meaning of the natural world. For Catholics, this discussion is inseparable from understanding human existence itself and our place in the cosmos, created by a God who loves us and knows us deeply.

Therefore, in light of the Catholic faith, the Theory of Intelligent Design is not only compatible, but also enriches the understanding of creation as an act of love and divine wisdom. By considering the natural world through the lens of intelligent design, Catholics find a fruitful dialogue between science and faith, sustaining the conviction that ultimately all creation points to its Creator, who sustains it in its being and the guide to his ultimate end.

# 8. IS IT POSSIBLE TO ACHIEVE IMMORTALITY (ETERNAL LIFE) WITHOUT GOD?

Since space travel, even at the speed of light, would take too long to be completed in a human lifetime, one solution would be for us to live forever; this way, there would be time to get to Andromeda, for example, explore at will and return to Earth (or stay there, enjoying some sulfuric acid beach). What's the problem with that? Well, where does God stand in this hypothesis?

The question of the possibility of achieving eternal life without God is deeply relevant to the Catholic faith and requires a careful understanding of the principles of Christian doctrine and revelation. For the Catholic Church, eternal life, understood as eternal communion with God in Heaven, is intrinsically linked to the personal relationship with God, who is the source and foundation of eternal life. Let's explore this topic from a Catholic perspective.

In Catholic doctrine, eternal life is the supreme gift that God offers to humanity. It is described as the full and definitive union with God, which is the Supreme Bliss and the final fulfillment of human existence. The Bible and Church teachings affirm that eternal life is a free gift from God, granted through grace, and not something that can be meritoriously achieved through our own efforts.

According to the Catechism of the Catholic Church, God is the "beginning and end" of all creation and redemption. Jesus Christ, the Son of God, is the mediator through whom humanity can attain eternal life. Through His life, death, and resurrection, Christ offers the way to salvation and eternal life. In the Gospel of John, Jesus states: "I am the way, the truth and the life; no one comes to the Father except through me" (John 14:6). This teaching emphasizes the centrality of Christ and, by extension, God in obtaining eternal life.

The Catholic Church teaches that Christ is the only Savior and that salvation is found exclusively in Him. The Second Vatican Council, in its constitution Lumen Gentium, declares that "outside the Church there is no salvation", although this is understood in an inclusive and mysterious way. This means that even for those who do not explicitly know the Christian message, God can work in ways that transcend human understanding to offer salvation. However, the Church affirms that the ordinary and safest means of achieving eternal life is the explicit acceptance of the message and grace offered by Christ.

However, the Church recognizes that people of good will, who seek the truth and practice justice according to their conscience (indigenous people, aborigines, people who have not had any patch of catechesis), can be touched by divine grace in ways that we may not fully understand. However, adherence to God and the sincere search for truth are seen as fundamental steps towards achieving the fullness of eternal life.

In the Catholic faith, achieving eternal life without God is not seen as a viable possibility, as eternal life is understood as full and eternal communion with God. Relationship with God is the central aspect of eternal life, and Christ is considered the only path to this communion. Although the Church recognizes that God can work in mysterious and inclusive ways, Catholic doctrine asserts that explicit adherence to Christ and acceptance of His grace is the ordinary and sure way to attain eternal life.

Thus, within the context of the Catholic faith, eternal life is inseparable from God and His revelation in Jesus Christ. It is, therefore, a gift from God, and it is through communion with Him that the fullness of happiness and existence is realized.

Based on this explanation, it is essential to make an important distinction: eternal life, union with God in a full and irrevocable way, IS NOT TO BE MISUNDERSTOOD with the immortality that many wish to achieve through scientific and technological progress.

In short, your body dies and you *upload* it to a machine, to continue (surviving) living (even if you can call that life, but let's move on).

Our soul is made up of four parts, the two lowest (which we have no control over) are imagination (creativity in the broadest sense) and memory (facts, feelings, even sounds and smells are recorded) and two highest, intelligence (logical, mathematical, linguistic, spatial reasoning) and will (inner strength, courage, wanting to accomplish something, achieve goals).

I imagine that in the near future it will be possible for equipment to save all the memories of a human being, something around 100 Terabytes, but it could be much more if all the crazy ideas that have crossed the person's head throughout their life are included, but she didn't pay much attention. That would be the memory part.

It is worth remembering that it is not easy to read and interpret an individual's neural synapses, which is why this technology has progressed, but in very short steps.

Let's also assume that this mechanism that stores memories makes combinations of different concepts that the individual has stored, from mixing mint with chocolate in an ice cream to more extreme sexual fantasies. Okay, we have a creativity based on trial and error, and probably more interesting than a lot of the nonsense available on social media today.

On top of all this, let's assume that this machine can reason and draw conclusions about concrete concepts like two plus two equals four, or even abstract concepts like "it's good to respect others", "it's bad to take someone's life"; just as a child learns these concepts and does not forget, the upload of a person's neural package must include all their understandings and positions about what is right and what is wrong, as they are the result of what we were taught and are stored in our memories.

But what about the will? Free will? This is intrinsic to each soul, and can never be recorded on a device. Within our decision-making process, the person (in theory) evaluates the best available course of action, based on the information they have, and often makes completely absurd decisions, which they know are wrong or harmful. But they go ahead, punching the tip of a knife, stubbornness combined with arrogance.

Many will argue then: we don't need free will, let's always make the best decision possible and not allow the self-sabotage that causes us so much suffering. It turns out that this idea has two problems.

First, without discernment we stop being human beings, we start to react like machines without the slightest pleasure or displeasure in living. What a mediocre little life, even if that can be considered a life.

Second, God created us this way, the immortal soul breathed into each of us at the moment of conception is what makes us human, free to decide between good and evil. This is what God wants from us, human beings capable of being saints, but also of throwing our souls into the eternal trash can, without the right to recycling.

Animals do not have free will, they react based on their instincts and memories. Of course, many animals reason and have a good deal of discernment (even more than many humans out there), but they are not capable of making decisions like human beings, created in the image and likeness of God, the only beings capable of loving and suffering, of sacrificing themselves for something greater than themselves, of renouncing this world in the hope of the next.

It is our immortal soul that makes us human beings, not our earthly experiences. It seems paradoxical, but it is not: suffering makes us human, it is the ability to decide between grace and sin, between virtue and vice, which allows us to approach the eternal, and even the misery of sin rooted in the soul can be able to provide a personal encounter with God.

In a nutshell, the supposed immortality that scientific progress promises to bring will degrade us to the condition of automatons, a little better than animals, but without sanctifying grace, incapable of acting in accordance with the motions of the Holy Spirit.

The staunch defenders of Artificial Intelligence can criticize me at will, I continue to maintain the position that this technology will only design machines capable of performing tasks (in this regard they are fantastic), adopting the best line of action according to the variables available (best than many human beings), but they will not acquire consciousness (and dominate the world).

But I don't rule out the hypothesis that AI will make people increasingly idiotic, incapable of logical reasoning or critical thinking, or even recognizing the truth before their eyes. Program a machine (or educate a man) to respond that grass is not green, or that two plus two do not equal four, and she (or he) will obediently respond as programmed, even if it leads to her self-destruction (together with mankind's extinction).

As you are reading this book now, instead of seeing nonsense on various social media that distract us from our life goals (personal, family, professional and especially spiritual), steal our precious life time and alienate us (aliens?) , know that you are a hero of resistance against the domination of machines over our thoughts. We stick together, bro.

After all, what fun is it to continue this existence for so long? "Which of you, however much he cares, can add one cubit to the course of his life?" (Matthew 6, 27). "Even the hairs on your head are all numbered" (Luke 12:7). No machine will be able to do what God did for us by giving us the gift of life. "Behold, I have engraved you on the palm of my hands" (Isaiah 49, 16).

Apparently, this trip to other planets is not easy at all, none of the hypotheses have been tested in technological and theological analysis. And please, don't tell me about spiritual trips to other planets... I don't know what you smoked to think that, but it wasn't a good thing. We will address this soon.

In conclusion, let's take care of our backyard, our pale blue dot in the Universe, created by God for us, and offer our efforts to obtain a better place in eternity. That's what we have for today.

# 9. ARE ALIENS (IF THEY EXIST) INCLUDED IN THE REDEMPTION BY CHRIST?

The question about the inclusion of possible forms of extraterrestrial life in the redemption offered by Christ is a fascinating and complex topic, which mixes theology, philosophy and science. In the context of Catholic faith, reflection on aliens and their relationship to redemption requires careful consideration of the principles of Christian theology, especially the universality of salvation and the role of Jesus Christ.

In the Catholic faith, redemption is a gift offered by God to humanity through Jesus Christ. The Catechism of the Catholic Church teaches that Christ, as the Son of God, came into the world to save humanity from sin and eternal death. Redemption is understood as a universal act of love and divine grace, intended for all human beings.

The incarnation of Christ and His redemptive death are seen as events that have a cosmic importance, not limited to Earth alone, but that have a dimension that transcends time and space. Therefore, the universality of redemption is a central principle in Catholic theology, indicating that the offer of salvation is intended for all humanity.

Recognizing the possibility of extraterrestrial life is not incompatible with the Catholic faith. The Church does not have an official position on the existence of life on other planets, but the fact that creation is vast and diverse enough opens up the possibility that other forms of life could exist. In 2008, Pope Benedict XVI stated that belief in the existence of extraterrestrial life is not contrary to the Christian faith and that the search for life beyond Earth can actually deepen our understanding of the greatness of God as Creator.

If we were to hypothetically encounter extraterrestrial life forms, the question of whether they are included in Christ's redemption is profoundly theological. The Catholic Church could consider several possibilities based on its doctrine:

1. **Universality of Redemption**: Catholic doctrine states that Christ died for the salvation of all humanity. If extraterrestrial life is found, the same logic could apply, with the possibility that the redemption offered by Christ is universal and encompasses all intelligent forms of life. The divine nature of Christ could have a reach that transcends the boundaries of time and space, beyond planetary limits.

2. **Inculturation and Redemption**: The Catholic Church teaches that the message of Christ must be inculturated in different human cultures. If extraterrestrial beings with their own culture and rationality exist, the principle of inculturation could extend to them, allowing the message of salvation to be adapted in a way that resonates with their own understanding and experience. The catechesis of the Jesuits in the Americas was exactly like this, since at the time there were not enough cultural elements for the Tupiniquins to understand the concept of sin and saving grace.

3. **Mystery of Salvation**: The mystery of salvation is a central theme in Catholic theology. If extraterrestrial life forms exist, the Church could consider the exact manner in which these life forms participate in redemption to be a mystery that belongs to divine wisdom and mercy. God may have means and ways of saving that go beyond human understanding.

4. **Christ and Creation**: In Colossians 1:16, it is said that "in Christ all things were created in heaven and on earth." This passage can be interpreted as indicating that Christ's redemption can extend to all of creation, not just the Earth. Thus, if extraterrestrial life exists, the redemption offered by Christ could somehow be applicable to them as well.

The inclusion of possible forms of extraterrestrial life in Christ's redemption is an issue that challenges the boundaries of theological and scientific knowledge. The Catholic Church, with its understanding of the universality of redemption, can consider the possibility that the salvation offered by Christ has a reach that transcends the Earth, making room for the inclusion of any form of intelligent life that may exist outside our planet.

Ultimately, the question remains shrouded in mystery and speculation, and the complete understanding of how redemption applies to any possible extraterrestrial life belongs to God's infinite wisdom. The focus of the Catholic Church remains on the importance of Christ's message for humanity and on the continuous search for truth and understanding of divine design.

In a way, we have excellent news: if there is intelligent life on other planets, we have a duty to evangelize them. "Go into all the world, preach the Gospel to every creature" (Mark 16:15). Any being endowed with an immortal soul, capable of discerning between good and evil, even if he has green skin and backward knees, deserves to know the message of salvation through Our Lord Jesus Christ.

Or do you think it was peaceful for the Jesuits when they arrived in America? Diseases, various dangers, communication difficulties. However, it was these pioneers of the proclamation of the Gospel of peace who lived and died to fulfill this divine order.

Now comes the bad news: even if you consider the immensity of the Universe, the possibility of finding life outside Earth is extremely low, and intelligent life is practically nil. This is a difficult truth for all science fiction fans to swallow, but the immensely greater probability is that it is just us, human beings here in Little Earth.

Does this mean that we will stop exploring other planets and distant celestial bodies? Far from it, I believe every penny spent on telescopes, space probes and all types of research is worth it, even to prove which of the theories of the origin of life on Earth is correct.

If God created the world, according to the Big Bang Theory created by Father Georges Lemaître and duly proven by Edwin Hubble with the observation that galaxies are moving apart, you can be sure that God's hand is present in the formation of life also, regardless of which theory prevails. One day, perhaps, God will allow us to also discover what He meant by "the breath of life in the nostrils of Adam", in Genesis, which granted us an immortal soul and made us the image and likeness of the Creator. Let us wait with faith and hope.

# 10. DID JESUS ASK US TO TAKE THE GOSPEL TO OTHER PLANETS?

This question mixes theological, speculative and science fiction elements. To address this topic, it is important to explore the historical and theological context of Jesus' messages and how these messages have been interpreted over the centuries.

Jesus of Nazareth, the central figure of Christianity, lived and preached in 1st century Palestine. His teachings and life are recorded mainly in the New Testament Gospels, which emphasize the message of salvation, love, and the arrival of the Kingdom of God. The Gospels record that Jesus gave a specific mission to his followers: "Go therefore and make disciples of all nations" (Matthew 28, 19), which is known as the Great Commission.

This mission was understood, within the historical context of the time, as a call to spread the teachings of Jesus to all nations and peoples on Earth. There is no explicit reference in traditional biblical texts to other planets or worlds besides Earth. The vision of the Great Commission was therefore interpreted as a command to expand the Christian message among the people of the Earth.

Did Saint Peter, Prince of the Apostles, have any idea that the Earth was round and that there were indigenous peoples in the Americas to be catechized too? Could it be. There is a story in Catholic tradition that Saint Thomas, the apostle of the lack of faith, set foot here in Brazil and preached the Good News of salvation to the natives, before leaving for the region that is now India, where he was martyred.

Reports from the discoverers of Brazil say that the foresters here in the Land of the Holy Cross, upon receiving the announcement of the Gospel and realizing the divine connection that the priests made through the Holy Mass, reported that a person called Zomé had already passed through these parts speaking of Jesus, and they even pointed to a stone on a beach, with a right foot marked on it, a sign that the apostle left when he came here for the first time. There is no scientific proof, only historical proof. Check out Raphael Tonon's explanation on the subject <https://www.youtube.com/watch?v=JLNNvUS9U3M>.

With the advancement of science and space exploration, the idea of life on other planets has become a real and intriguing possibility. Although the Bible does not directly mention other planets, some theologians and scholars speculate about the reach of divine messages in a vast universe.

Science fiction often explores similar themes, creating scenarios where religions and teachings are adapted to extraterrestrial contexts. These scenarios offer a way to imagine how spiritual and ethical principles could apply in a broader universe, but these representations are ultimately speculative and not based on traditional religious texts.

1. **Universal Mission x Local Mission**: The message of Jesus, as recorded in the Gospels, is often interpreted as having a universal character in the sense that it should reach all nations on Earth. The idea of taking the gospel to other planets is not mentioned directly, but can be seen as a speculative extension of the idea of a universal message.

2. **Modern Interpretations**: Some modern theologians and philosophers may explore the idea that the Christian message could have implications for universal understanding, including the possibility of extraterrestrial life. However, these interpretations have no basis in ancient texts and are more a matter of speculation and philosophical reflection.

3. **Spiritual and Scientific Exploration**: Space exploration and the search for extraterrestrial life open new questions about how we understand our place in the universe and how we apply our spiritual and ethical principles. Although there are no explicit mandates to evangelize other planets, the search for a deeper understanding of the universe can enrich our spiritual vision.

Although the idea that Jesus sent the gospel to other planets is not found in Christian traditions or biblical texts, it offers an interesting opportunity to reflect on the reach and depth of the Christian message in an expanding universe. The Great Commission, as traditionally understood, is a call to spread the message of love and salvation among the people of the Earth. Speculation about other planets is a fascinating exercise at the intersection of faith, science, and imagination, but, to date, it remains in the realm of speculation and science fiction.

# 11. THE TRUTH IS INSIDE HERE

The search for truth is one of the distinctive characteristics of the human experience, encompassing both science and theology. In the Catholic tradition, scientific and theological truth are seen as distinct paths that, although they operate in different spheres, can interact and complement each other. The Catholic faith offers a unique framework for understanding how these two forms of knowledge relate to and influence each other.

Science seeks to understand the natural world through observation, experimentation and analysis. Scientific methods are based on collecting empirical evidence and formulating theories that can be tested and refined. The Catholic Church has a long history of involvement with science, including figures such as Saint Thomas Aquinas, who integrated scientific and philosophical knowledge into his theological thought, and Saint Albert the Great, patron saint of natural sciences.

The Church has always recognized the validity of the scientific method and the importance of scientific discoveries in understanding how the universe works. From the earliest days of modern science, many scientists were also devout Catholics, such as Gregor Mendel, the father of genetics, and Georges Lemaître, the priest and astronomer who formulated the Big Bang theory. Louis Pasteur, pioneer of microbiology and inventor of the rabies vaccine, prayed the Rosary devoutly, and did not let the Enlightenment of the time contaminate his thinking or his faith (https://fr.aleteia.org/2019/01/24/le-jour-ou-louis-pasteur-demontra-que-science-et-foi-etaient-compatibles).

Theology, on the other hand, is the study of divine revelation and the relationship between God and humanity. Catholic theology is based on Scripture and Tradition, seeking to understand God's plan for the world and salvation. The Catechism of the Catholic Church and the works of the Church Fathers are primary sources of theological knowledge.

For the Catholic Church, theological truth is revealed by God and accessible through faith and reason. Theological truth is not a simple human construction, but a discovery of the divine plan, which is considered absolute and immutable.

The Catholic faith teaches that science and theology, although distinct, are not in essential conflict. The Catholic Church sees both as ways of seeking truth and believes that they can coexist and complement each other. This view is based on the belief that truth is ultimately one, and that both science and theology seek to understand different aspects of the same reality.

The Catholic Church defends the idea that science and theology address different dimensions of reality. Science explores the "how" of the natural world, while theology seeks to answer the "why" of existence and purpose. Pope John Paul II's Encyclical *Fides et Ratio* states that "philosophy and the sciences are situated in the order of natural reason, while faith, illuminated and guided by the Spirit, recognizes in the message of salvation the fullness of grace and truth ( Jn 1, 14) that God wanted to reveal in history, definitively, through his Son Jesus Christ (1 Jn 5, 9; Jn 5, 31 and 32)".

Dialogue between science and theology can lead to a richer understanding of truth. Scientific understanding of the origins of the universe, for example, can enrich the theological view of creation, while theological reflections can offer perspective on the limits and purposes of science. The Church encourages this dialogue, as it believes it can promote a more complete and harmonious vision of reality.

When apparent conflicts between science and theology arise, the Catholic Church seeks to resolve them through an approach that respects the integrity of both disciplines. Rather than viewing conflicts as battles, the Church views them as opportunities to deepen understanding and adjust theological interpretations in light of new scientific discoveries.

History offers several examples of how the Catholic Church reconciled science with theology. The case for the heliocentric theory, defended by Galileo Galilei, initially encountered resistance, but was eventually and carefully integrated into the Catholic understanding of creation. More recently, the acceptance of the Big Bang theory and biological evolution (as already explained in the Chapter about the Theory of the Intelligent Design) within the Church demonstrates the ability to adapt and enrich theology as new scientific evidence emerges.

The biblical text of Genesis 1:3 illuminates the human mind from the beginning: "God said: let there be light! And the light was made." BANG! First day. Now we understand at least what this cosmic explosion was like, which simply detonated all the accumulated energy of the Universe and set everything in motion. A BIG of a BANG! Contradiction? Only in your head!

The discovery of truth, both scientific and theological, is an ongoing effort that seeks to better understand the universe and humanity's place within it. The Catholic faith offers a context that sees science and theology as fields that, although distinct in their methods and objectives, can collaborate and enrich each other. The Church believes that by seeking truth with humility and openness, human beings can come to a deeper and more complete understanding of reality, reflecting the unity and integrity of divine creation.

The final scene of the film "Star Trek – The Last Frontier" is very interesting, because it illustrates this thought well. In the film, a renegade Vulcan named Sybok is looking for a way to reach the center of the Milky Way and find God. If you don't mind, there are spoilers in the following paragraphs.

In short, Sybok hijacks the Enterprise and takes everyone to coordinates 0 – 0 – 0 – 0, the center of the Milky Way. There he encounters a very strange entity, who entitled itself God, who asks the spacecraft to get closer to understand how the travelers overcame the galaxy barrier (i.e. intergalactic travel). Captain Kirk questions the supposed God asking how an Almighty and Omniscient being neither knows nor can overcome the barrier of the galaxy, and needs a spaceship.

After many proton beams on the embezzler alien who wanted to pretend to be God, doctor McCoy asks Captain Kirk: "So that means God doesn't exist?", and the answer was worth all the clichés in the film so far: "Actually, Bones (McCoy's nickname), **he's among us**." End of the film.

Who knew that, even with so much scientific and technological progress, the character Captain Kirk still believed in God? And did you know His Word? Who would have thought that a film that marked an entire generation of scientists, scholars, inventors and nerds of all kinds would quote a biblical passage (Luke 17, 21)?

Know yourself, this is the invitation of John Paul II in *Fides et Ratio*. We don't need to travel the galaxies to find the truth. She's in here. She is in our midst.

# 12. CONCLUSION

Does God exist? Yes, that we know. Believe whoever wants.

Did God create the Universe? Yes, that we know, there is enough scientific proof.

Did God create life on Earth? Yes, we have evidence in this sense, God's signature is present in every form of life, and in all creation (Wisdom 13, 5).

Did God create man in his image and likeness? Believe it or not, we are not the result of chance.

Is there life outside Earth? We don't know. Intelligent life? We don't know. The only certainty is that, if it exists, God created it. I will deliver this incomplete answer.

Was Jesus an alien? No, He was born here, from the Virgin Mary, by the work of the Holy Spirit of God. Jesus existed from the beginning (John 1:1).

Are miracles advanced and unknown forms of technologies? I highly doubt it, because God accomplishes the impossible without needing to satisfy anyone. The chariots of fire described by Ezekiel (Ez 1) and Elijah (2 Kings 2, 11), the guiding star of the Magi (Matthew 2, 1), are nothing more than visible interactions of supernatural elements that observers were able to witness.

What about alien metals to build spaceships? Now, go study Chemistry! Where these people come from...

Will we be able to obtain enough energy to make intergalactic trips through Quantum Physics? Max Planck would be amazed to see how everyone uses the word "quantum" to give more credibility to their product or service. Study a little Physics and you will understand.

Is heaven a place? Yes. Is heaven a state of mind? Yes.

Is it possible to reach heaven? Yes, uniting with God through prayer, asceticism, the sacraments, especially the Holy Eucharist.

Saint Maria Faustina Kowalska's mystical experiences with Jesus make it clear that there is a profound interaction between heaven and earth, between material reality and supernatural life. In addition to the Apostle of Divine Mercy, so many young people had encounters with Our Lady in so many places around the world that it is possible to say three things:

- there is a huge support in another existence for each of us to get there too (salvation is for everyone, John 10, 10);

- there is also the group of those excluded from God's grace, who spend all eternity trying to bring more people to their team;

- sooner or later we will have to embark on one of these two routes, a one-way route. Will you wait to book the ticket the day before, when the ticket becomes more expensive?

And with a spaceship? Even if one day humanity manages to overcome the tremendous technological challenges of an intergalactic journey, upon arriving at the eternal home the traveler will find "angels with fiery swords guarding the place" (Genesis 3, 24).

In other words, you cannot enter the party without an entry ticket. The last one who tried to enter the party without the appropriate clothing (state of grace, union with God) had his feet and hands tied and thrown out into the darkness (Matthew 22, 15). Will you face it?

Is there any passage in the Bible that talks about aliens? This answer is more complex, and necessary to avoid false interpretations of the Word of God.

Without a shadow of a doubt, the Bible mentions non-human intelligent beings, creatures with full knowledge of revealed truth and capable of knowing and determining Good and Evil. They are the angels of God and the fallen angels. But they are not the only intelligent creatures found in biblical texts.

The Nephilim are an enigmatic figure mentioned briefly in the Bible, specifically in the Book of Genesis. Although its role and nature are not entirely clear, Catholic tradition offers some interpretations and contexts that help understand its place in the biblical narrative. We will conceptualize the Nephilim in the light of the Catholic faith, addressing their origins, interpretations and theological implications.

The most direct reference to the Nephilim is found in Genesis 6:1-4:

*"When men began to multiply in the earth and daughters were born to them, the sons of God saw that the daughters of men were beautiful; and they took wives for themselves from all they chose. Then the Lord said, 'My Spirit will not he will contend with man forever, for he is flesh; but his days will be one hundred and twenty years.' In those days the Nephilim were in the earth, and also afterward, when the sons of God went to have relations with the daughters of men and children were born to them. These are the mighty men who were of old, the men of fame."*

This passage is the only one in the Bible that explicitly mentions the Nephilim, and is accompanied by a series of interpretative questions and debates about their true nature.

In Catholic tradition, a common interpretation is that the Nephilim were giants or beings of extraordinary stature. This interpretation is based on ancient translations of the word "nephilim" as "giants." The expression "the mighty men who were of old" is often seen as a reference to mythical or legendary figures of antiquity, known for their greatness and heroic deeds.

Another interpretation is that the "sons of God" and the "daughters of men" refer to two different lineages: the descendants of Seth (the "sons of God") and the descendants of Cain (the "daughters of men"). According to this view, the Nephilim would be the descendants of these unions, described as great heroes or warriors who stood out for their achievements.

Some traditions and apocryphal texts suggest that the Nephilim could have been fallen angels or supernatural beings who interacted with humanity in a corrupt way. This view is most common in apocryphal literature, such as the Book of Enoch, which details the story of the "watchers" – angels who descended to Earth and took human wives, spawning a race of giants. Although it is not part of the official canon, this tradition influenced some interpretations about the Nephilim, which have long been discarded for a very simple and obvious reason: angels do not procreate (they don't even have defined sex, come on).

The Catholic Church, in its official interpretations, does not adopt the view of the Nephilim as fallen angels, since this is an interpretation more associated with non-canonical texts. Instead, Catholic tradition tends to focus on the idea that the Nephilim were notable and powerful figures in antiquity, recognizing the ambiguity and symbolism present in the biblical text.

In the Catholic tradition, the central message of the account of the Nephilim is not so much about the nature of these beings, but about the consequences of human disobedience and corruption. The text of Genesis 6 is interpreted as a preamble to the Flood, which is seen as a divine response to the increase in evil and corruption on Earth. The presence of the Nephilim is therefore yet another way to highlight the decadent moral environment that led to God's judgment.

The Catechism of the Catholic Church does not provide a specific doctrine about the Nephilim, but it emphasizes that the truth revealed in Scripture must be understood within the context of salvation and Christian morality. The Church's focus is on how these biblical texts reveal aspects of human nature and the divine plan, rather than on specific details about enigmatic figures.

The Nephilim remain an enigmatic figure within Catholic tradition, with interpretations ranging from legendary giants to powerful figures from ancient times. Although the Catholic Church does not have a detailed dogmatic position on the Nephilim, it does offer a view that places them within the moral and theological context of Scripture. Ultimately, the account of the Nephilim serves as a backdrop for reflecting on human nature, disobedience, and divine judgment, highlighting the importance of justice and righteousness in the history of salvation.

Most biblical scholars argue that the Nephilim and the sons of God in Genesis can be understood as a reminiscent reference to the mythology of the creation of the world by the pagans who lived with ancient Israel, and were written by that type of person whose culture saw any someone who was not from their tribe as being strange (alien comes from the Latin Alienus, foreigner, which comes from outside, which is why foreigners and aliens can be used as synonyms).

Whether these creatures are angels or aliens does not really matter to our argument here. The crux of the matter is that the ancient writers of the Bible, like all ancient people, did not even consider the possibility of the existence of other intelligent beings, because they were humble enough to recognize how limited their knowledge was. The world was a big place, most of it unknown and probably hostile. They had no idea that the Earth was round.

It is a fact that this God, revealed to his chosen people, who created all these other creatures, has a special loving relationship with his people: the people of Israel and, through the redemptive work of Christ, all humanity became "children of God", that Jesus managed to make us, in the words of Saint Paul (Romans 8, 17) "co-heirs" of his Kingdom.

For Jesus to have come to this pagan world, God first needed to form a people who believed in the one God (not in the people who idolized the Sun, animals, volcanoes, and various paganisms) and within these people choose the perfect woman for His Son (What childhood would Jesus have had it if Our Lady had been born or lived in Persia or Babylon?).

Thus, the children of God were the Israeli people, and the children of men were the pagan people. All human beings, descendants of Adam and Eve.

In fact, it was only in the "enlightenment" of the 18th century that skepticism towards the existence of other creatures took hold. Even today, the scientific study of life in the universe has to fight hard to overcome the prejudice in our modern culture that extraterrestrial beings are nothing more than invention or superstition.

Many of the stories told by pioneers traveling the world at that time may have been true, but the overwhelming majority were mere fabrications. You cannot fight a superstition with another superstition, but only with the truth.

Science has to correct the superstitions of its time. In turn, as Pope John Paul II's statement states, religion must also remind us of the limits of our scientific knowledge.

The point of this entire discussion is simple. There is nothing in Holy Scripture that can confirm, or contradict, the possibility of intelligent life in other parts of the universe. We don't know. We are free to speculate.

But this speculation finds its limits in two crucial principles of our faith. First, whatever is out there was created by a God of love. And second, no matter what God does or doesn't do with the rest of creation, nothing we discover will contradict what we know He has done here for us.

Can we take spiritual trips to other planets? Seriously, do you really want me to talk about this?

In the context of the Catholic faith, which is deeply rooted in tradition and the revealed doctrine, this concept is approached with a critical and reflective eye. Although the Catholic Church does not specifically address spiritual travel to other planets, some theological and spiritual principles can offer a perspective on how to consider this idea.

The Catholic Church bases its doctrine on Divine Revelation, which includes the Scriptures and Tradition. The Catholic faith teaches that God created the universe and everything in it. The Catholic view of the cosmos is one of order and purpose, and creation is seen as a reflection of divine greatness and plan.

The Catechism of the Catholic Church emphasizes the importance of prayer and meditation as means to draw closer to God and better understand His plan for humanity. However, the idea of spiritually traveling to other planets is not a practice or concept formally recognized by the Church.

In other words, in the Catholic tradition there are no spiritual journeys, but rather MYSTIC EXPERIENCES, in which the saints had visions or supernatural experiences. These encounters often have a symbolic dimension and are seen as ways in which God reveals aspects of His will or His presence.

For example, Saint Teresa of Ávila and Saint John of the Cross, Carmelite mystics, speak of profound spiritual experiences that transcend the limitations of space and time. However, these experiences are interpreted as visions of spiritual reality and not as physical or literal journeys to other worlds.

Saint John Bosco, with the help and protection of his guardian angel, had mystical experiences that led him to glimpse heaven, hell and purgatory, which he described and is in a book with this title. He glimpsed it at a glance, because these are places in which God does not allow excursions or camping. Read the book and see: what the Apostle of Youth saw was not a hallucination, so much so that when the expedition ended, the palm of his hand had serious burns, just for having touched the gate to the kingdom of perdition.

Many saints had the gift of bilocation: Felipe Neri, Catarina de Ricci, Pedro de Alcântara, Afonso Maria de Ligório, Antônio de Pádua, the Brazilian Frei Galvão and Padre Pio traveled to other cities and countries and returned at the same time. Saint Rita of Cássia, after a moment of ecstasy, miraculously appeared inside a convent. What would prevent them from visiting other planets? Simple.

The bilocations occurred so that the saints could do GOD'S WILL in their lives, not out of mere curiosity. The intention in all cases was to SAVE someone's SOUL, through the saint. Understand at once: knowledge for knowledge's sake brings no sustenance to the soul. Agnosticism has already caused many people to stumble, unfortunately.

Prayer, meditation and the sacraments are the means by which Catholics seek a deeper union with God and a greater understanding of His creation. The great mystical experience that every Catholic must seek is found in the Eucharist, because through the Sublime Sacrament we can, at least for a moment, touch the supernatural plane, the world up high (even if at first it only touches the up high of the mouth).

"My flesh is food indeed, and my blood is drink indeed" (John 6:56). Some pagans were anthropophagous (cannibals), while Catholics are Christological (eucharistic). However, pay attention to an important detail: "Therefore, everyone who eats the bread or drinks the cup of the Lord unworthily will be guilty of the body and blood of the Lord" (1 Corinthians 11, 27).

Important: to have an excellent experience with Jesus at Holy Mass, it is necessary to have spiritual preparation (sincere confession, Eucharistic devotion), which begins as soon as you decide to go to Church that day. I'm going to give you an important tip: stop following the Mass through the leaflet, it doesn't make sense to look at a piece of paper while the sky is revealing itself on the altar, at the moment of the consecration.

How to explain the stigmata of Padre Pio, Saint Rita of Cassia, Saint Francis of Assisi? All the doctors who checked the open wounds of the Saint of Pietrelcina (as it was the most modern case, medicine was well advanced at the time, capable of proving whether it was a fake or true), had to bow to the miracle (or at least the inability of finding an explanation for a wound that does not heal, does not become infected and does not mutilate the patient even though it lasted fifty years).

Is it possible to find an explanation for the Eucharistic miracles, such as Lanciano, Santarém, Buenos Aires, Tixtla, Sokolka and Legnica? In all of them, the same results: AB+ blood, human DNA, white and red blood cells indicating that the person is alive, tissue from a human myocardium, taken from the left ventricle of an inflamed heart, with signs of having gone through supreme anguish.

The scientific explanation in all cases is that there is no scientific explanation. The answer to this mystery we find only on the path between Gethsemane and Golgotha. "Deny yourself, take up your cross and follow me" (Matthew 16, 21).

Following Jesus is not only in ideal conditions of temperature and pressure, but the true Christian is with Christ on Calvary. This mystical experience is priceless, but it comes at a very high cost. "For to live for me is Christ, to die for me is gain" (Philippians 1, 21). Right path to heaven.

In this sense, mystical experiences can be seen as an inner journey towards greater communion with God and a greater understanding of His plan. These journeys are guided by faith and spiritual practice, and are seen as paths to personal and spiritual transformation.

Unfortunately, there are many people pretending to be mystics just for personal gain, money, fame, status, etc. "Each tree is known by the fruit it produces" (Luke 6, 44). True mystics, on the contrary, sought poverty, anonymity and even humiliation, because they did not want to run the risk of losing heaven because their egos were inflated by pride.

Mystical experiences are very personal, they are often an event between the person and God, such as the miracle of the smile between Our Lady and Saint Therese of the Child Jesus (the miracle of the Sun, in the last apparition of Fátima, witnessed by thousands of people, is exception). I'll leave you with some examples that happened to me:

- when taking a public exam, I started praying the rosary before starting the tests, and even without having studied some subjects, while reading the questions the important parts were automatically illuminated, which helped me a lot to be approved;

- in the second test of this same public exam, I stopped the rosary in the fourth mystery and opened the test, only to discover that the words were all jumbled up; I resumed the rosary, prayed the last mystery and the Hail Queen; when I opened it again, the letters were in order, even illuminating the questions to show that they would be null;

- when I was returning from a mission, I accidentally ended up going to the wrong airport. I took a taxi and said a rosary as well, explaining that I wouldn't be able to change the ticket. That day the flight was delayed four hours, the only delayed flight of the day, and I managed to board on the last call;

- I was sleeping at home alone early in the morning when a voice called me loudly: "Rogério!", and I woke up just in time for an important appointment;

- on more than one occasion, driving in the rain at night, I avoided an accident because I had the Rosary in my hands, praying even without much devotion.

In fact these are small miracles compared to everything that happens in our lives, how God gave us this wonderful gift and everything related to it. As Chesterton already argued, children see miracles because they still have the ability to marvel even at the monotony of life. *"It may be that He (God) has an eternal childhood appetite; for we sin and grow old, and our Father is younger than us. Repetition in Nature may not be a simple recurrence; she could be a theater BIS. Heavens may have asked for BIS from the little bird that laid an egg."*

Wonders exist, we are the ones who become dry at heart and lose the ability to marvel. "*Truly I say to you, unless you convert and become like little children, you will not enter the kingdom of heaven.*" (Matthew 18, 3). For a heart of stone there is no mystical experience enough, but for an open heart all existence is a gift from God, a wonderful experience even when washing the dishes.

The Catholic faith offers a context for reflecting on the relationship between the spiritual and the material, the known and the unknown. The Catholic view of the universe is a creation ordered and guided by God, and spiritual experiences are understood as paths to deepen the relationship with the divine.

Catholic spirituality invites believers to explore the deeper dimensions of reality through prayer and meditation, always seeking a greater understanding of the divine plan and creation.

The greatest and most important journey that human beings can achieve is the personal encounter with God, the most sublime experience for our soul. This mystical journey requires much more than scientific or even theological knowledge (many saints were illiterate, but they had a wisdom that would make many university professors envious), it requires a life of prayer, asceticism, devotion, sacraments... in short, seeking the things from above (Colossians 3:1).

You can build an excellent spaceship through your spiritual progress, obtained by knowing God and knowing yourself. Be yourself a rocket to heaven, built with virtues and powered by the strength of the Holy Spirit. This is the great journey of our lives.

If God allows, we will meet there. Have a good trip.

###

This book represents the author's opinion and nothing more; it does not represent the views of any government, organization or third party.

Likewise, it does not contain sensitive or confidential information. I always play by the rules.

Thank you for your interest in reading this book. My sincere thanks.

Certainly many people will not agree with him, as is common in any discussion... Therefore, I would like to know your point of view.

Feel free to send suggestions, comments and opinions to rogeriocietto@gmail.com, Subject Were the Saints Astronauts?. Your email is very welcome.

Other published books, available in the main online bookstores, in different languages:

- Armor of the Christian – Preparation and engagement in spiritual combat

- Ecolar – A holistic vision of sustainable living

- The Lion and the Dragon – a fictional tale about economics and politics

- Fighting the good fight – how to fight terrorism with a peace mission

- The fuse of the rifle – terrorism as a legal framework for the application of International Humanitarian Law

I regret to inform you that you will not find me on Facebook, Twitter, Orkut or any other social media.

Some information about me:

Academic Training

1998 - 2002 - Graduated in Law.

Itu Law School, Faditu, Brazil

2004 - 2005 - Postgraduate degree in Tax Law.

Itu Law School, Faditu, Brazil

2008 - 2008 - Postgraduate degree in Complementary Applications to Military Sciences - Law.

Army Administration School, EsAEx, Salvador, Brazil

2009 - 2010 - Postgraduate (Specialization) in International Humanitarian Law

HUMANMED Program - Université de Nice, France

2011 - 2012 – Professional Qualification in Peace Operations

Peace Operations Training Institute, United States of America

2016 – 2016 – Military Senior Officer's Course

Brazilian Senior Officer's School

2018 – 2019 – Postgraduate in Military Law

University Center South of Minas, Brazil

2020 - 2021 – University Master in DDHH, DIH and Operational Law

Antonio de Nebrija University, Spain

Military Organizations I've been:

2008 - Army Administration School, Salvador, Brazil

2009 – 8th Military Region, Amazon Rainforest, Belém, Brazil

2010 – Amapá Border Company, Oiapoque, Brazil

2011 – Department of Engineering and Construction, Brasília, Brazil

2012 – Brazilian Battalion in Haiti, Port-au-Prince, Haiti

2013 – Special Operations Command, Goiânia, Brazil

www.ingramcontent.com/pod-product-compliance
Lightning Source LLC
LaVergne TN
LVHW040956150826
845672LV00002B/723

* 9 7 9 8 2 2 7 2 2 0 1 9 6 *